Ancient Magick for Today's Witch Series

WICCAN BASICS

MONIQUE JOINER SIEDLAK

Wiccan Basics © 2015 by Monique Joiner Siedlak

All rights reserved

The content contained within this book may not be reproduced, duplicated or transmitted without direct written permission from the author or the publisher.

Under no circumstances will any blame or legal responsibility be held against the publisher, or author, for any damages, reparation, or monetary loss due to the information contained within this book, either directly or indirectly.

Paperback: 978-1-948834-70-4

EBook: 978-1-948834-12-4

Legal Notice

This book is copyright protected. It is only for personal use. You cannot amend, distribute, sell, use, quote or paraphrase any part, or the content within this book, without the consent of the author or publisher.

Disclaimer Notice

Please note the information contained within this document is for educational and entertainment purposes only. All effort has been executed to present accurate, up to date, reliable, complete information. No warranties of any kind are declared or implied. Readers acknowledge that the author is not engaged in the rendering of legal, financial, medical or professional advice. The content within this book has been derived from various sources. Please consult a licensed professional before attempting any techniques outlined in this book.

By reading this document, the reader agrees that under no circumstances is the author responsible for any losses, direct or indirect, that are incurred as a result of the use of the information contained within this document, including, but not limited to, errors, omissions, or inaccuracies.

Cover Design by MJS

Cover Image by MidJourney

Published by Oshun Publications
www.oshunpublications.com

ANCIENT MAGICK FOR TODAY'S WITCH SERIES

The *Ancient Magick for Today's Witch Series* is a series for modern witches to explore ancient magick, covering Celtic, Gypsy, and Crystal magic, among others. It offers practical advice on spells, rituals, and enchantments for today's use, incorporating natural energies and spiritual connections. With insights into Shamanism, Wicca, and more, it helps readers enhance their magickal journey, offering paths to protection, prosperity, and spiritual growth by combining ancient wisdom with contemporary practice.

Wiccan Basics

Candle Magick

Wiccan Spells

Love Spells

Abundance Spells

Herb Magick

Moon Magick

Creating Your Own Spells

Gypsy Magic

Protection Magick

Celtic Magick

Shamanic Magick

Crystal Magic

Sacred Spaces

Solitary Witchcraft

Novice Witch's Guide

MONIQUE JOINER SIEDLAK

GET UPDATES, FREEBIES & GIVEAWAYS

JOIN MY NEWSLETTER

MOJOSIEDLAK.COM/MOONLIGHT-MUSINGS

CONTENTS

Introduction   xiii

1. Is Witchcraft Wicca?   1
2. Basic Beliefs   7
3. Gods and Goddesses   19
4. The Witch's Pyramid and Elements   25
5. Tools of the Craft   29
6. Witch's Calendar   35
7. Ceremonies, Rites, and Rituals   41
8. Moon Phases   43
9. Days of the Magickal Week   45
10. Magickal Colors   51
11. Herbs of the Zodiac   53

Conclusion   55
References   57
About the Author   61
More Books by Monique   63
Don't Miss Out   67

INTRODUCTION

It is a popular misconception that everyone who practices Wicca is a witch that practices magic, or that every Pagan is a Wiccan. Yes, it can get very confusing, and these practices are usually always misunderstood as dark arts or practices of those who worship Satan. But nothing can be removed from the truth.

While there are those who practice the dark arts such as black magic or Hoodoo, most Pagans, Wiccans, and witchcraft don't include this. They have definite rules and credence that followers of these crafts follow. This book has been written to assist readers looking for spiritual guidance into the world of Paganism and the Wiccan culture.

Paganism has been around in some form or other for thousands of years and pre-dates most religions, including Christianity. Paganism is believed to have its roots in Animism (Perkins, 2019). Animism is thought to date back to the Paleolithic period and prehistoric man or hominids (National Geographic Society, 2012).

The Animism belief is that inanimate and animate objects all have an essence or spirit (soul). It is this essence or spirit which connects or binds all things around us together. It is the foundation upon which most modern-day spirituality, beliefs, and even religions are built upon. (Perkins, 2019)

Paganism is a term that incorporates non-Abrahamic faiths and usually worships two deities like a God and a Goddess (ditheistic). They may also worship more than one God or Goddesses (polytheistic). Wiccans all fall under the Paganism umbrella, and although some Wiccans practice forms of magic, they are not evil.

The best way to understand Wicca is by learning about the practice and its comparison to other practices. This book will escort you through the basics of the Wiccan ways, their traditions, and rites.

1

IS WITCHCRAFT WICCA?

It is quite the problem of figuring out what or if there is a difference between Witchcraft and Wicca. Although they are usually lumped together as the same, they are not.

This chapter looks at Paganism, Witchcraft, and Wicca to help you better understand these practices.

Pagan Times

Pagan times refer to pre-Christian religions, where the people believed in a series of Gods and Goddesses. Greek Mythology is Paganism, as is Roman Mythology, Norse Mythology, and Egyptian Mythology. The people of these times worshipped the various Gods and Goddesses known to these ancient myths, using them to explain different aspects of life around them. For instance, in ancient Greece, women would take offerings to Demeter's shrine, the Goddess of harvest and agriculture or fertility. This would be every spring to ensure good crops and a successful harvest. A poor crop would have the farmer believe that they had somehow displeased her.

The word Pagan was mentioned in ancient text and came from the Latin word paganus, which, when translated, means country dweller. A country dweller refers to a location where many shrines were set up and used to worship the mythical Gods and Goddesses of the times. The word was only used to refer to non-Abrahamic faiths to differentiate them from Christian, Islam, and Judaism religions by writers of the Medieval and Renaissance eras. Because the term Pagan appeared in some ancient texts referring to these places of worship, it was mistakenly believed to reference a religious sect.

Hellene was the correct word used during the rise of Christianity in the eastern communities to refer to those who did not follow the Christian faith. They were called Hellene because the people from Hellas were more resistant to Christianity and remained loyal to their Gods and Goddesses. Hellas was what the ancient Greeks called Greece.

Back in the times when Abrahamic religions arose, there was a lot of strife between Christianity and Judaism. As politics and religion intertwined, it was easier to define a person's religious beliefs by their ethnic origins. This meant that those who worshiped Roman Gods were called Romans, and followers of Norse Gods were called Norsemen.

The word Pagan was not used until the 1400s. During those historic times, the term was used to condemn people who did not follow an Abrahamic faith. They were thought of as sinful or that they worshiped the devil and used witchcraft. Pagans became targets for anything bad that happened to a village, and they were often sentenced to odious deaths. Through ignorance and prejudice, the word Pagan and heathen meant the same thing for centuries. Practitioners of various Paganistic faiths were mistakenly lumped with those that had no faith or beliefs at all.

It is only now, in modern times, where people have broadened their minds and accepted that some other beliefs do not conform to the mainstream ones. That by grouping Paganism with non-believers and various other heathen type sects is derogatory to the Pagans.

So what exactly is Paganism? It is the term that embraces practices or faiths such as:

- Wicca
- Druidism
- Eclectic Witchcraft
- Asatru
- Thelema
- Reconstructionism
- Dianic
- And a lot more

To break it down more, a Wiccan is a Pagan, but a Pagan is not necessarily a Wiccan and may follow another Pagan faith.

Witchcraft

Witches are practitioners of witchcraft, which is more of a skill set than religion, or part of their spiritual beliefs or practices to some people. Being a witch does not entail having to interact with the Divine. A person can be a Christian and still practice witchcraft, which is why there is a Christian witch movement. There is also Jewitchery, which is the practice of Jewish mysticism. There is also the atheist witch, who does not follow a deity, eclectic witches, and more.

There are no hard or fast rules that bind any religion or spiritual practice to witchcraft. Some Pagans practice witchcraft as part of their religion or spiritual practices. Some Pagans do not practice witchcraft at all. Some Pagans practice witchcraft separately from their religion or spiritual practices—it is more of a skill set.

Witchcraft is not all about magic powers and pacts with the devil. Some practitioners believe in the dark arts, black magic type ritual sacrifices, and Hoodoo type practices. But that is not what most modern witchcraft practices are about, and it is a far cry from modern witches' beliefs.

In past times, healers used various herbs and harnessed the powers of the Gods or Goddesses of their times to strengthen their healing powers. Healers in villagers back then were mainly wise older women who would pass their knowledge of herbs onto their daughters or granddaughters. They often called upon these healers to draw help from their deities to heal and ensure good crops and prosperity.

But the very people they helped also feared these healers. To the villagers, the healers could destroy just as easily as they healed. When things did not go so well for the people, and poor crops would lead to starving villages, sickness, and chaos, magic arose. Wise older women became known as crones—practitioners of magic who cast spells and sent strife upon the townspeople. As a result, the witches or those perceived as witches were shunned and hunted, forced to live as outcasts in isolation or hiding.

Modern-day witches practice as either solo witches or belong to a coven or some spiritual group. While there are various spells that witches use, they are mostly to draw those positive energies towards the practitioner or negative energies away from them. Some witches make various tinctures, ointments, creams, teas, and salves from herbs, plants, and flowers.

Most modern-day witches live by strict belief, rules, respect for all things, and believe that anything done to someone else comes back to you tenfold. Different sects have different rituals, rites, and beliefs, but they all follow the fundamental rule to do no harm.

Wicca

Wicca is a form of Paganism introduced to the world in the 1950s by Gerald Gardner. Although there is much debate about it, Wicca ideally embraces an ancient practice of witchcraft being based on the traditional practices, rituals, and so forth.

While not all Pagans or witches are Wiccans, all Wiccans are Pagans who follow some form or an ancient traditional form of witchcraft. They respect nature, the Gods and Goddesses they may follow, and are strict with their rules, with one of the crucial ones being to do no harm.

The Wiccan movement has followers worldwide but is more predominant in Europe and the United States of America. Thanks to actions founded by Gerald Gardner, witchcraft was molded into what it has become in today's world. Wiccan covens worldwide allow people to express their spirituality that is not bound by mainstream religious sects. It is a lifestyle that embraces nature, deities of the ancients, and practices magic following the ways of the coven.

While Wicca has its root in witchcraft, not all witches are Wiccan, just like not all Pagans are Wiccan or witches.

2

BASIC BELIEFS

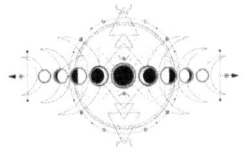

Wiccan practices are more predominantly found in the Western world. There are no specific ways of Wicca, which allows for the great diversity in which it is practiced amongst the different Wiccan sects.

Although the Wicca religion arose in the 1950s, it was not until 1986 that Wicca was identified as an official religion in the United States. Thanks to the rise of the new green and healthy lifestyle movement that has arisen in the past ten years, more individuals are shifting to Wicca or Paganism (Zilber, 2018).

Wiccan Practices

Within the past six to seven decades, the Wiccan religion has developed into many forms, each with their spin on how to practice their ways, making it hard to generalize Wiccan practices and beliefs.

There are no written texts defining precisely what the religion is or how followers of the religion must think or how they should practice their art. However, there are core components to the Wiccan religion woven into, and that shape the basis of every coven or solitary Wiccan.

Many forms of Wicca are practices, with some of the more popular ones being:

- Alexandrian Wicca
- Celtic Wicca
- Dianic Wicca
- Discordianism or Erisian
- Gardnerian Wicca
- Georgian Wicca
- And more

Wiccan Rede

The Wiccan Rede is a guideline of rules and ethical standards that Wiccan covens or sects follow. There are a few unique interpretations of the Wiccan Rede in circulation since the first one published by Gerald Gardner came out. However, the Rede has individual clarifications for different sects most, if not all Wiccan sects abide by the basic principles of the document.

The most familiar form of the Wiccan Rede is Lady Gwen Thompson (Wigington, 2018):

Bide the Wiccan laws ye must,

in perfect love and perfect trust.

Live and let live, fairly take, and fairly give.

Cast the Circle thrice about

to keep the evil spirits out.

. . .

To bind the spell every time,

let the spell be spake in rhyme.

Soft of eye and light of touch,

speak little, listen much.

Deosil go by the waxing Moon,

sing and dance the Wiccan rune.

Widdershins go when the Moon doth wane,

and the Werewolf howls by the dread Wolfsbane.

When the Lady's Moon is new,

kiss thy hand to Her times two.

When the Moon rides at Her peak

then your heart's desire seek.

Heed the Northwind's mighty gale;

lock the door and drop the sail.

When the wind comes from the South,

love will kiss thee on the mouth.

When the wind blows from the East,

expect the new and set the feast.

When the West wind blows o'er thee,

departed spirits restless be.

. . .

Nine woods in the Cauldron go,

burn them quick a' burn them slow.

Elder be ye Lady's tree;

burn it not or cursed ye'll be.

When the Wheel begins to turn,

let the Beltane fires burn.

When the Wheel has turned at Yule,

light the log and let Pan rule.

Heed ye flower bush and tree,

by the Lady Bless'd Be.

Where the rippling waters go

cast a stone and truth ye'll know.

When find that ye have a need,

hearken not to others' greed.

With the fool no season spend

or be counted as his friend.

Merry meet and merry part,

bright the cheeks and warm the heart.

Mind the Threefold Law ye should,

three times bad and three times good.

When misfortune is enow,

wear the Blue Star on thy brow.

True in love ever be

unless thy lover's false to thee.

Eight words ye Wiccan Rede fulfill:

An' it harms none, do what ye will.

Respect for Nature

Wicca is a belief system based around nature, which most sects personify as Father Sky and Mother Earth. Most of the Wiccan movements strongly believe that nature, or more accurately, the universe, is Divine and deserves the utmost respect. All things come into existence because of nature and the universe. A deep respect for the Earth and all it has birthed is the backbone of the Wiccan religion.

Wiccans mostly believe that a person's strength and faith in themselves can be restored by connecting to nature. Taking a walk barefoot through the grass, or sitting on it, or communing with nature in any way can release negative energies within oneself.

In the Wiccan culture, there are many ways that nature can cure, heal, and bring peace to one's soul.

Wicca also draws from the four elements of nature. These elements also represent certain aspects of a human being.

The four elements of nature are:

- Air—In humans, this element represents the mind and imagination, intelligence, and psychic abilities. It is a masculine element that can be represented by the Wiccan faith with smoke, the sky, or even a feather.

- Earth—In humans, the Earth is a feminine element and represents strength, prosperity, plants and herbs, stability, and nurture. The element earth is usually shown with symbols or images made from either stone or wood.
- Fire—In humans, fire represents love, passion, ambition, courage, desire, strong will, and inspiration. It is masculine energy and is symbolized by burning candles or a controlled fire such as bone fires.
- Water—Represents purification, wisdom, emotion, calming, and healing. Water is feminine energy represented by pouring water, dousing, ritual bathing, or a body of water.

The Pentagram

Contrary to popular belief, the pentagram in Wiccan belief is not evil, nor does it represent good versus evil. Instead, the pentagram is a symbol of the Wiccan faith and represents the five elements with the circle representing the universe connecting and containing them.

Each point of the five-pointed star of the pentagram represents one element which are:

- The spirit—The top point of the star.
- Air—The point of the star to the left of the spirit element.
- Earth—The point of the star beneath the air element.
- Fire—The point of the star beneath the water element and next to the earth element.
- Water—The point of the start to the right of the spirit element.

Another grave misconception is how the fifth point of the star points makes the pentagram good or evil. Wicca can use the symbol with the point pointing up or down. It is most commonly used with the top point of the star pointing upwards, which symbolizes the spirit element ruling over the other four elements.

Pentagram as word comes from the Greek words:

- pente which means five
- graphein which means to write

When the terms are joined to form "pentagram," they can either mean a star or an object made up of five lines.

The pentagram symbolizes the four elements of nature and the element of the spirit and embodies the number five as a sacred number. It is a number found all over nature and in many life forms. For instance, flowers, the human hand, the human body, starfish, and many more. The number five can be seen as the essence of life itself. The patter of the number five exists right down to the molecular level of life forms, making it the foundation of their existence.

Wiccans also use the pentagram as a protection against evil, in any form like keeping out evil spirits during rituals or spells. It can also keep negative energy at bay or from polluting one's Karma. Most people who wear a pentagram, do so because they are at one with nature and can feel its presence in everything. They also wear it out of respect for nature and the infinite universe.

The pentacle is the pentagram symbol enclosed in a circle representing infinity.

The pentagram represents the Wiccan faith, and no matter which way the star points, in Wiccan religions, it never represents good or evil.

To the Wiccan faith, the pentagram pointing upwards is part of certain initiations or rituals. They use it for "second-degree initiations," which shows that the person being initiated has turned the spiritual journey inwards. The star pointing upwards represents "the spirit descending into the matter" (K, 2018). It is a journey into conquering inner fears and overcoming prejudice, anger, ignorance, and establishing control over one's base emotions.

The pentagram can ward off negative energies and invoke positive ones during ceremonies, rituals, and rites. Wiccan use it as a symbol for protection during their sacred times and find it a source of comfort on spiritual journeys.

Two Wiccan sects rarely use the pentagram in the same way for their practices.

Gender Identity

Wicca is a religion that strives to obtain a balance in all things. Thus, during Wiccan rituals, the practitioners are usually individually inscribed with both feminine and masculine identities. Regardless of a person's sex or how they identify themselves as a gender, each individual has to embrace both masculine and feminine energy.

It is untrue that Wiccan or Pagan practices are purely for women. The reason most Wiccan are women is that witchcraft and spiritualism appeal more to the female sex. Not that there are not those of the male persuasion that are not Wiccan, because there is and the male numbers rise each year.

However, most Pagan beliefs indeed embrace the feminine as sacred with the masculine as power. There is a definite polarity to the Pagan faiths that appeal to women. Most women in a male-dominated world turn to Wicca, as they feel more powerful and in control as they embrace the masculine and the feminine.

There is no gender bias in the hierarchical, or rather, leadership structures of Wiccan sects. As Wiccan and many other Pagan faiths were born from religions that honored fertility and held it in the highest regard, they hold the feminine in high relation. Some Wiccan sects only recognize one Goddess or God. Most Wiccan faiths honor both to seek perfect balance and harmony within nature and the universe. Although there are few rites and rituals that would not seem right for a man, like the ones about the womb, there is a different context for each that men can adjust these to.

We Do Not Convert

Wicca is a practice that does not hate other religions. It respects the rights of a human being to have their own faith and beliefs. Wiccans also do not take part in vulgar animal sacrifices or other types of horrific sacrifice type rituals. They do not believe in, worship or interact with Satan/the Devil. Satan or the devil forms part of the Christian religion.

Unlike Christians and most other religions, Wiccan does not believe in proselytizing. Wiccans believe that the spirit is free to choose its own path, so you will not see them going door to door trying to preach the word of their Wiccan sect. They will not attempt to convert a person to their ways, and they do not prey on the vulnerable, indoctrinating them into religious cults.

Wiccans mostly view proselytizing for what it is—a form of bullying—and coercing a person into believing in something.

Instead, Wiccans believe that if a person is meant to become a Wiccan, they will find their own way to the faith. It is a calling from the soul, echoed by a deep connection to the universe around all living things. There is also nothing in the Wiccan way of life that prevents one of their followers from having more than one religion or belief system.

Wicca encourages people to establish their power in their own life. Practitioners of the faith believe it is more important to figure out what best suits you and not what the world expects you to think think.

The Wiccan faith does not convert their members; they accept members who are looking for spiritual enlightenment and finding their own paths to their awakening. You will not find pamphlets stuck on windshields of your car, or shoved into your post box, or have a Wiccan knocking on the door. You will not find them displaying enormous billboards or other similar signs telling when their next meeting is. Nor will you find them preaching the end of world scenarios and why you should join their covens.

To find a coven takes a bit of research, and then you have to establish contact with the coven. Unlike different sectors of the same Christian based religions, you will not find the different covens ever judging you, wanting to follow the other covens' ways. They will never try to change your mind about what you believe, but they expect you to show theirs the same respect.

Afterlife

Unlike other religious groups, Wiccans do not pretend to know what happens after death. There is also nothing documented or set in stone about how the different Wiccans groups should view what happens after death. However, there are a few unique views or beliefs that can be found in certain Wiccan sects.

Some Wiccan views on the afterlife include:

- Reincarnation—Wicca looks at life as cyclical, meaning that everything in life is recycled. For instance, the changing of the seasons, the phases of the Moon, and the soul or spirit is eternal. Therefore, as a person finishes one life, they will eventually move on to their next life.
- Free spirits—In some Wiccan beliefs, the soul, being eternal, once freed from the confines of the human body, can travel the vast expanses of time and space. Once free of its mortal coil, the spirit can choose to be born again, walk the earth in its non-corporeal form, or travel to where no earthbound being can.
- Trapped spirits—In some Wiccan beliefs, spirits can become trapped or earthbound. This can happen when a soul has unfinished business, negative energies around them when they die or do not know or accept they are dead. Not until these souls are somehow freed from whatever binds them to that plane can they move on and be reincarnated, get to the Summerlands, or roam the universe.
- Becoming one once again with the Great Divine—There are Wiccan faiths that believe after being reincarnated a few times, the soul is eventually ready to be absorbed and become one with the Great Divine. Moving beyond having a body of flesh and bones, past wandering through the spirit world, and rejoining the Great Divine. In Wicca, it is believed that everyone comes from the Great Divine and shall someday return to the Great Divine.

- Summerlands—The Summerlands should be unmistaken for the Wiccan version of heaven. It is not; it is a place that some Wiccans believe exists on another plane. This world is a spirit world where spirits go to rest once they are done with the earthly plane. It is the place that exists behind "the veil" and where spirits go to reunite with those they lost or met through their life's journey(s) (Wright, 2020).
- There are Wiccan faiths that believe there is nothing after death; that is it; it is the end. A person's light goes out, the universe reabsorbs their energy, and their body becomes one with nature.

3

GODS AND GODDESSES

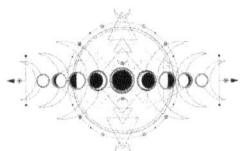

Wiccan faiths usually have more than one deity as they seek universal balance in all things, including that of the feminine and masculine. Thus, both male and female deities in the sects that recognize more than one will give equal emphasis to both.

As most covens will have their own sacred names for their deities, they are generally referred to as "the God" or "the Goddess." However, some common deities are recognized throughout Wiccan practices.

Horned God

The Horned God is also recognized as "the God" and is the ancient God of fertility, protector of the children, and "the Goddess" herself. The Horned God reigns over life, death, and resurrection, just as he is both light and dark.

He represents all that is masculine in the Wiccan religion and is usually referred to as "the God" with close associations to the sun. This could be why he may be referred to as Father Sky.

The Horned God has a dual role in life as he protects both the hunter and the hunted as he keeps the delicate balance of nature. There are few rituals or rites where Wiccan faiths that are polytheism sects will not honor, draw from, or give thanks to the Horned God.

Green Man

The Green Man is a sacred Wiccan God of the woodlands. They usually depict this God with horns and found looking out at the world through the sacred oak or other foliage, which he sports as a mask.

They worship the Green Man as the God of vegetation, and he offers the mystic energy of nature.

Sun God

The Sun God is a masculine deity and evokes youth, beauty, and light. The Wiccan faith draws on the Sun God to offer them wisdom, spark inspiration, and help them heal. Wicca will call forth the power of the Sun God to bless them with light and fill them with warmth.

Triple Goddess

The Triple Goddess has the starring role as the supreme Goddess in Wiccan faiths. They also know her as the Moon Goddess, who represents divine feminine power. She is the physical energy representative of the earth and all that springs to life on it. Her being surrounds every living creature and thing on the planet as it is her essence that nurtures it.

The Triple Goddess blesses all unions between partners, friends, and even those of domesticated animals. While the Green Man or Horned God may protect the crops and watch over them while they grow, the Triple Goddess nurtures them to their full potential.

The Triple Goddess is throughout the cycles of life and can adapt to all changes. She is the Goddess that keeps the Wheel of the Year going around. She sweeps away the old and makes sure the new is ushered in like the dawn that lights each fresh day.

The Three Aspects of the Triple Goddess

There are three main aspects of the Triple Goddess. They can be perceived as a whole or single deity depending on the cycle of the Moon.

Maiden

The Maiden is seen as one aspect of the Triple Goddess that represents new beginnings, youthfulness, and sexuality. The Maiden is evoked when looking to bring about changes, new beginnings, and fresh starts.

The waxing phase of the Moon is associated with the Maiden, and it is during the period that her essence is the strongest to draw upon.

Mother

The Mother is another aspect of the Triple Goddess, and her essence is the strongest during a full moon. The Mother is associated with the giving of life. She is called upon for blessings of fertility, stability, inner peace, motherhood, and intuition. The Mother also offers protection for the practitioner and her family.

Crone

The waning of the Moon is associated with the least liked and most misunderstood aspect of the Triple Goddess—The Crone. The Crone makes people think of death, witches with ugly warts on their nose, and aging. While she is associated with aging and death, she is by no means a witch with warts. They call upon the Crone for spiritual guidance because of her vast knowledge and universal wisdom. She is the one that gives a person the strength and courage to face often hard endings.

Still there are others do not believe in the gods as real personalities, yet attempt to have a relationship with them as personifications of universal principles or as Jungian archetypes. Some Wiccans conceive deities as similar to thought forms.

DIETY

OFFERINGS

SYMBOLS AND IMAGES

ALTAR TOOLS

CANDLES COLORS

THE GODDESS

PURPLE OR WHITE FLOWERS, OLIVE OIL, HIBISCUS, CHAMOMILE

A CIRCLE FLANKED BY TWO CRESENT MOONS

CUP, PENTALE, BELL, CAULDRON

BLACK, WHITE, SILVER, GREEN

MAIDEN

WHITE WHINE, PINK FLOWERS

WAXING MOON, DEER, OWL

AMETHYST, CLEAR QUARTZ, ROSE QUARTZ

WHITE, PINK

MOTHER

HONEY, MILK, ROSES

FULL MOON, CAULDREN

BLOODSTONE, ROSE QUARTZ, GARNET

RED

CRONE

APPLES, RED WINE

WANING MOON, LANTERN, KEY

JET, OBSIDIAN, ONYX

BLACK

THE GOD

Bread, basil, clover, pine needles, fruit

A crescent moon on top of a circle

Censer, wand, athame, boline

Gold, red, orange, yellow, green

THE HORNED GOD

Cheese, pine cones, nettles

Horns, spears, swords, arrows

Bloodstone, green tourmaline, tiger's eye

Green, gols

THE SUN GOD

Sunflower seeds and petals

Sun, flames

Sunstone, citrine, carnelian

Red, orange, yellow

4

THE WITCH'S PYRAMID AND ELEMENTS

The Witch's Pyramid applies not only to Wiccan witches. It is a perspective that is based on most witchcraft practices. It also contains concepts that can be used in typical aspects of a person's life.

The pyramid lists the steps to achieving affecting magic, and traditionally it only contained four elements. The fifth element is a newer element introduced by various covens, and each coven that incorporates the fifth element may perceive it differently.

Nescere: To Know

This step refers to the witch being consciously aware of what they are about to do. They must have weighed up all the consequences of their actions.

To be fully aware of what they are about to do, the witch must consider the following:

- Know their desires and that of others.
- Understand their desires and those of others.

- Know their craft and everything that is needed.
- Make sure there is always a balance.
- Make sure they fully understand what the costs may be to themselves and others.

Velle: To Will

The witch needs to understand and act on what they need right now rather than what they want. They must be able to will what they want by being able to meld their emotions, energies, and thoughts together. To will something to take the witch's utmost concentration and the manifestation of their will.

To be manifest their will, the witch needs to consider the following:

- Make sure they understand the difference between want and need.
- To carefully consider their wants, needs, and desires.
- Be able to distinguish between the surface and true desires.
- Have clearly defined objectives and goals.

Audere: To Dare

A witch needs not only to will their needs into manifestation. They need to be able to follow-through. This is the strong intention to make it happen no matter what, which brings about the concept "To dare it to be so." Often a person is the one standing in their own way of getting what they want.

To manifest their will, the witch needs to consider the following:

- Make sure they understand the difference between want and need.

- Have faith in their abilities to bring about their will and to make it happen.
- Have the courage to conquer fear, and whatever is holding them back.
- Have the time, energy, and be able to put in the effort to live their dream.

Tacere: To Keep Silent

To keep silent does not mean to have your Wiccan faith or that you practice witchcraft a secret. It implies that spouting off about your magic and spells mixes them with the negativity, prejudices, and scorn of others. Being able to keep silent about your rituals gives the witch an inner strength and keeps their magic pure.

Keeping silent for the witch means taking the following considerations into account:

- Never brag about the magic you have done.
- Never use magic for greed.
- Never try forcing magic on another person.
- Only talk about magic to those wanting to hear about it.

Ire: To Go

Once the spell is performed, the witch has raised the four powers of the Magnus. To go means that the spell should now "go" out to the universe, and if it was performed correctly, there will be results. They associate this step of the pyramid with the spirit. It is the moment the energy of the spell flows out to the universe, guided by the hand of the witch.

Ire considerations:

- How easy is it to visualize what needs to be done?
- Did the energy flow easily from soul to fingers?
- At any point, was something blocking the flow of energy?
- If the spell was performed before, how well did it work?
- Was full attention given to the manifestation of desire and the workings of the spell?

5

TOOLS OF THE CRAFT

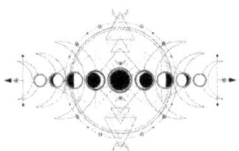

It is essential to know that your magickal tools do have a physical function. Before you decide to go out and acquire one, you need to learn just what this is. These tools are often characteristic of one of the four standard elements, which might help you decide on the tool you want for your intention.

Many Pagan beliefs use subsequent tools in specific roles, but not everyone does. If you don't feel that you need a particular item, don't feel obliged to use it in your method.

Cauldron

The cauldron is a classic pot or vessel for cooking and brewing. A depiction of the Goddess, the cauldron is sole regarding femininity. Life develops in the belly. Even though it usually represents the water element, the cauldron is out of the conventional tool since it can be associated with the four elements. The cauldron can be placed on top of the Earth, heated up using Fire, filled with water, and, finally, directs the steam with Air's help. The Goddess Cerridwen, In Celtic legend, had a cauldron of immortality and creativity that signified transformation, in addition to femininity and fertility. The cauldron is regularly used as the focal point of the ritual because of its functional structure. Customarily, cauldrons are made of cast-iron and have three legs.

In selected traditions, a chalice or cup is used instead of a cauldron; also, other traditions, a cauldron, and a bowl are handled simultaneously. A cup is simply a little cauldron that can be constructed of any substance.

Chalice

The chalice is a cup. In ancient times it was made of gold, silver, pewters, or specially carved from the sacred wood. It used to perform rituals with and represents fertility. During the Great Rite, it is used in conjunction with the athame.

Signifying the Goddess, fertility, and corresponding with the element of Water, the chalice accomplishes the same purpose as the cauldron, but in smaller proportions. It can be for holding saltwater to cleanse objects with, mixing potions, or holding ritual wine or any other liquids.

Wand

The Wand has been utilized for thousands of years as a vital magick tool. As commonplace as it may be, the wand is one of the most universal magickal tools in Wicca and in some ceremonial magick traditions. It has several magickal purposes. A wand is used to focus on energy during a ritual, drawing circles and creating magickal symbols. Because it's a phallic symbol, it is used to represent male power, strength, and potency. It is associated with the symbol of Air, a sacred element of the Gods. Wands are customarily constructed from elder, oak, or willow. However, practically any substance can be used to make a wand. Now and again, crystals are added to the ends of wands, seeing as crystals increase the energy sent throughout the wand. The wand can be used to bless a sacred area or to call upon a deity.

Athame

Pronounced "a-tha-may," the athame is dagger or magical knife used in rituals, rites, and spells. It is not used to cut anything. The athame would traditionally have a hard black or dark handle. It has a double edge dull blade used to direct energies, casting a circle, and to manipulate power during a ritual. You may engrave your athame with magickal symbols, but it really is not necessary. It is a ceremonial knife instead of a functional one. Connected through the element of Fire, the athame is a phallic sign and is used as a symbol of the God.

Boline

The boline is a knife or dagger with a sharp single sickle-shaped edge and a white handle. This knife is used for cutting herbs, flowers, and other things that may be needed for potions, rituals, etc. The boline can be used both inside and outside your circle.

Pentacle

The pentacle is a five-sided star surrounded by a circle. It is used to ward off negative energies and project positive energies and keep practitioners safe from bad spirits when performing their art.

The pentacle is used as a protecting talisman. Yet, in most Wiccan traditions, it is seen as the natural element of Earth. It can be used on the altar to hold items that are going to be ritually consecrated. Crafted from any material, including wood, brass, gold, silver, clay, and wax, the pentacle is a tool of protection and a tool used for invocation. At times, the pentagram is thought to be a gateway between this world and the spirit world. From time to time, it is hung above windows and doors due to its protective qualities.

Nearly every tradition of Wicca (and many Pagan paths) uses the pentacle as a symbol. The most commonly seen symbol is the pentagram itself, which is why the two terms are often confused.

Besom

Commonly known as the Witch's broomstick, the besom is the witch's sacred broom and embodies both the Goddess and the God. The purpose of the besom is to clean and purify the surroundings before any rite, rituals, or acts of magic are performed before and after. A light cleaning not only cleans the natural area but also removes negative energies that might have been gathered in the space since the last cleaning. The broom is also a filter, so it is linked to the Water element. The traditional magickal procedure consists of a bundle of birch twigs, a staff of ash or oak, and a bind made from willow wands.

Censer

The censer is where the witch places incense to burn during rituals or magic practices. The censer is used similarly as a priest swinging a censer full of incense during mass. The censer holds smoldering incense through a ritual or ceremony. It can additionally rest on a table or swing from a chain. You can also use a small plate, bowl, or a cup with sand or salt to hold your incense. In many Wiccan customs, the incense represents the Air element.

Bell

Centuries ago, country people recognized that loud noise pushed away evil spirits. Also, the bell is a good noisemaker. It is usually a small handheld bell that is rung before and after rituals or some spells. The bell-ringing causes vibrations, which are the source of high power. Adaptations on the bell include the shaking of a sistrum, a singing bowl, or a ritual rattle. Each of these can help create harmony in a magickal circle. Some Wicca practices use the ringing bell to initiate or end a ceremony or call up the Goddess. It can also be used to welcome entities that may have been called upon into the practitioner's sacred circle.

Candles

When there are no candles in use, many Pagan ceremonies do not really feel complete. With some traditions, one candle is used to signify the God and an additional one used to signify the Goddess. In others, the candle is used to be a sign of the Fire element. Candles are frequently a tool in sympathetic magick rituals; besides, they can signify individuals, thoughts, and emotions. A basic candle magick spell consists of choosing a candle centered upon color correspondences, then engraving it with occult signs known as sigils and anointing the candle with the proper oil. Some Wiccans will burn candles that match the color of the day of the week.

Book of Shadows

Notwithstanding what the media may assume, there is no one single Book of Shadows. A book of shadows, or BOS, happens to be a Wiccan or Pagan's journal. It usually contains spells, rituals, correspondence charts, and information about the magick's rules, invocations, runes, myths, and legends of various pantheons. It can be an actual journal or saved to a computer. From time to time, the information in a Book of Shadows is given to one Wiccan to another in a coven setting, where there may be a coven Book of Shadows and individual members' books. The Book of Shadows is a unique item and should hold the most basic information, and you can design your own with a little bit of work.

Some get passed down for generations from one witch to another. Each generation will add their version of spells, rituals, and so on to the book. For new witches, they get to start and create their book of shadows. This they can pass on to someone they want to when the time is right.

Don't forget an important step, which is usually overlooked. All tools should be ritually cleansed, consecrated, and charged.

6

WITCH'S CALENDAR

Wheel of the Year festivals represents the active and passive states of nature, man, and cultivation. Each of the festival periods was ruled by a ruling deity, whether a God or Goddess, with each part having its own related deity. From sowing to reaping to winter to summer... the seasons were of vast importance to our ancestors, for their very survival rested on fruitful harvests, moderate winters, and adequate rainfall.

What is a Sabbat?

On the Wiccan Wheel of the Year, eight holidays are celebrated by witches. These holidays are known as Sabbats, which they celebrate from sundown on the day of the holiday to sunset the following day.

The following days are for the Northern Hemisphere. The Southern Hemisphere will celebrate some holidays like Summer Solstice and Winter Solstice, opposite to that of the Northern Hemisphere.

Accordingly, November 1st is really midnight on October 31st through November 1st. Likewise, the dates given here are only pertinent in the northern hemisphere. For the southern hemisphere, Sabbats usually are 6 months off from the standard dates.

Yule - Winter Solstice

While Christmas, Kwanzaa, and Hanukkah may indicate the month of December, it's time to celebrate Yule for pagans. The festival marks the Northern Hemisphere's Winter Solstice as the start of the Sun's return, and darkness changes into light

At that point, the Sun comes to its southernmost position in the sky, resulting in the year's shortest day, where the daylight hours are at their smallest. It is the start of the increasing daylight hours until the Summer Solstice, also called Saturnalia, when the night takes over once more.

Imbolc

Imbolc is the start of Spring and the arrival of the Sun. It is the holiday celebration of the end of winter, the commencement of the agricultural season, and the coming light half of the year.

This celebration also marks the renewal stage of the threefold Goddess powers from those of Crone to Maiden. She is a triple Goddess, so we celebrate her in all her phases. This is a time to connect with her and take care of the lighting of her divine flame. At this time of year, Wiccans will burn numerous candles, white for Brigid, to remind us of winter and the passage into Spring. This is an excellent time for initiations, whether they are they into covens or self-initiations.

Also Known As Brigid's Day, Candlemas, Groundhog's Day

Ostara - Spring Equinox

Spring Equinox marks the Spring Equinox. This is the Pagan "Easter" - or rather, this is the day that Christians adopted to be their Easter. It is generally the day of symmetry, neither bitter winter nor the relentless summer. In the old days, Ostara was a season of sowing and growing. Today, Ostara is a chance for setting projects into motion, sowing the grains of ideas that may not attain success for many months. Decorated eggs, baskets of blossoms, and such are commonly utilized to adorn the house. As a period of symmetry, it is an excellent time to perform self-banishings and perform workings to obtain elements we have lost or to obtain qualities we long to have.

Beltane

Otherwise known as May Day, May Eve, or Walpurgis Night, Beltane is one of the most significant Sabbat after Samhain, Beltane is the start of Summer. It is another fertility festival, but mostly, it is a festival of life and enjoyment. Named symbolizing the Celtic fire god Bel, the igniting of fires is a common element of Beltane events. The association with fire also causes Beltane a festivity of purification.

It officially starts at moonrise on May Day Eve and marks the start of the third quarter or second half of the ancient Celtic year. Contact with the fire was taken as symbolic contact with the Sun. In early Celtic days, the Druids would ignite the Beltane fires with specific incantations.

Litha - Summer Solstice

Also known as Midsummer or St. John's Day, the Summer Solstice, another fire festival, is the most important day of the Sun God. It is a celebration of development. The element of Fire is the most clearly identified and instantly felt element of transformation. It can burn, consume, cook, yield light or purify, and bonfires still figure prominently in modern Midsummer celebrations. It is a day for rejoicing, but also of meditation, making specific plans are still on course and correcting your life's negative situations.

Most societies of the Northern Hemisphere mark Midsummer in some ritualized form, and from time ancient people have recognized the rising of the Sun on this day. At Stonehenge, the heel stone records the midsummer sunrise as viewed from the center of the stone circle.

The use of fires and providing magickal aid to the Sun were also used to drive out evil and produce fertility and prosperity to men

It is the longest day of the year, illustrating the God at full strength. Although the warmest days of the summer still remain ahead, from this moment onward, we go in the waning year, and each day the Sun will withdraw from the skies a little sooner, until Yule, when the days start to become longer again.

Lammas

Lammas, also called Lughnasadh and Lughnassad, is the launch of autumn and is the stage of the first harvest. This is a festival of fulfillment and of preparedness for the coming winter. It is a time of gratitude for all that we possess, all that we will own, and all that others who have sacrificed for us.

The influence of the Sun extends into the grain as it ripens. It is collected and made into the first fresh bread of the fall. There are many practices and customs all over the land that are still carried on at harvest-time now.

Mabon - Autumn Equinox

Mabon marks the heart of the harvest. It is a moment of equal day and equal night. It is a time to receive what you have grown, expressing thanks for the harvest and the bounty the Earth gives.

Technically, an equinox is a celestial point and, because in actuality that the Earth bobbles on its axis somewhat, the date may fluctuate by a few days depending on the year. The autumnal equinox appears when the Sun crosses over the equator on its clear course southward, and we encounter a day and night that are of equal duration. Until Mabon, the hours of sunlight have been more significant than the hours from sunset to dawn. However, from now until the Spring Equinox, the reverse holds correct.

Samhain

The correct pronunciation is not sam-hane, but saw-win, saw-vane, sowen, or soween. Samhain is considered the Wiccan's New Year as well as the Feast of the Dead. It is a day to praise and say goodbye to loved ones who have crossed on, mainly if their deaths took place last year. Samhain is moreover an occasion for reflecting upon the previous year, creating plans for the approaching one, and specifically for eliminating weaknesses or other undesired aspects within us. Samhain is a cross-quarter day, set in the middle of the Autumn Equinox, in addition to the Winter Solstice.

Samhain gives rise to the Winter season. It is the last opportunity to dry herbs and save for winter, and a night when fairies produce mischief. Comparable to the Egyptians, the Celts, and ancient Mexicans, it is the Day of the Dead. The night when we recall our loved ones and worship our ancestors.

Samhain is known by many names such as Ancestor Night, Apple Fest, Candle Night, Day of the Dead, Devil Night, Feast of the Dead, Hallowe'en, Halloween, Hallows, Hallows Eve, Hallowtide, Harvest Home, Mischief Night, November Eve, Oidhche, Shadow Fest, Shamhna, Spirit Night, and Summer's End.

7

CEREMONIES, RITES, AND RITUALS

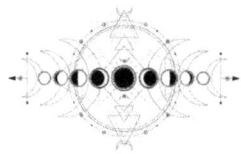

Wiccans celebrate the Sabbats. They cast circles, create magic, and worship their deities. Each coven will have their own form of rites, rituals, and the way they perform their ceremonies, but that is all based on a type of ancient practices. Each coven or solitary practitioner holds their rites, ceremonies, and rituals sacred; they keep this secret to the inner circle.

As each coven has its way of practicing, the most important thing to know about ceremonies, rites, and rituals is that each represents the Wiccan faith.

Ceremonies

Ceremonies are usually devotional, giving thanks and praise to their deities. It can be a handfasting ceremony for the joining of two coven members in a Wiccan marriage. They are usually performed on each of the Sabbats to mark the start of the holiday before the celebrations begin. Ceremonies can be done with magic, rituals, and rites.

Rites

Rites and rituals are closely intertwined with each other. They are both ritualistic. However, a rite is aimed more at a single person than a group. As with most Wiccan covens, each has its own set of rites. Usually, rituals performed to welcome new members. Rites can also be performed for members who are transcending to another level in their spiritual journey. In a handfasting ceremony, the partners being joined each has different rites they need to go through.

Rituals

Rituals are more structured types of ceremonies that are usually performed at the start of the covens gatherings. They are used for smudging to clear the air of negative energy or evil. Rituals are used to draw the cone of power, setting up the altar, drawing the protective circle, and more. Each coven has a unique set of sacred rituals that can be elaborate or subtle, peaceful, and straightforward. Most solitary practitioners will use more simple ritual practices.

8

MOON PHASES

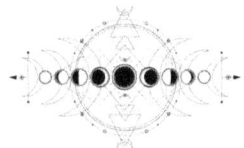

New Moon

When the Moon is unseen, also called the Dark of the Moon, it is the most influencing time to cast spells relating to new beginnings. It is normally a time to seize new paths and creating new plans started on the foundation of past events. The impact of the New Moon can furthermore increase your dreams and professions, so it is a beneficial time to planting the seeds of achievement. For the period of the New Moon, you will find that abundance spells, and employment spells have an improved possibility of being achieved than at other times. The New Moon is also commonly a suitable time to take a chance the future and spending currency and those who have undergone difficulties ought to take use of this indispensable phase.

Waxing Moon

The phase in the middle of the New Moon and Full Moon is the Waxing Moon. This is a distinctive period for gathering strength, development and growth. It is likewise a fitting time for arranging your magickal spells for the best favorable time, with that being the three days prior to the Moon is reaching full. The waxing Moon helps the achievement of any actions, whether of an everyday or spiritual temperament. For pagans/witches it is a period for pursuits, approval and a time in which to improve our magickal powers and our awareness of the other world. Actually, the closer we move towards the Full Moon, the greater and more ambitious are our instinctive power, which brings a new stage of mindfulness.

Full Moon

The Full Moon is the best opportunity time, particularly when it's drawing near Midnight, the witching hour. Your magickal powers and inner strength will be at their greatest. If you want more love in your life, this day is the time to send your wants into the universe. The Full Moon is furthermore the best fitting time to give appreciation and to pay honor to the spirits that protect and guide you. Through this time, the outgoing characteristics of our personality begin to appear more extrovert and open towards others. Use this period intelligently and develop your spells into gratifying practices.

Waning Moon

This is the phase when the Moon travels from Full to New Moon. Casting spells for doing away with trouble, defeating enemies, removing problems, and producing harm is most effective when the Moon is waning. Protection spells for yourself, your loved ones, home and material possessions are best cast at this time. It is also a time when our bodies are more susceptible to cleansing, so it is a good time to cleanse yourself through the process of detoxification. This can be best accomplished by way of healing and herbal remedies. You will find that diet and exercise likewise turn out to be easier in the course of this time with the results having a tendency to last longer.

9

DAYS OF THE MAGICKAL WEEK

Some witches, mostly Wiccans, do their spell work on certain days of the week, depending on the subject of the spell. They believe that the day of the week holds a special importance to the spell work.

Since the numerous gods control them, each week day creates an energy that is the best type of magickal working. The following is a list, which despite the fact is not completely comprehensive, will offer you a number of ideas of when to execute your spells.

Sunday

Traditionally the first day of the week and ruled by the Sun, it personified as Apollo, Bel, Beli, Helios or Lugh. In some traditions, the Sun is seen as feminine, personified as Phoebe in East Anglia, and Saule in Eastern Europe. The Sun rules the conscious element of the human mind, the ego, the "real" self." Sunday is the day on which this power is most effective.

Gender: Masculine

Color: Yellow

Planet: Sun

Element: Fire

Energies: Ambition, Goals, Career, Children, Fun, Health, Law, Success, Personal Finances, Promotion, Selling, Volunteers, Civic Services

Monday

This is the sacred day of the Moon, personified by such goddesses as Artemis, Diana, Luna, and Selene. The Moon is the ruler of flow affecting the changeable aspects of people. If a full moon falls on a Monday, its powers are at their most potent. Magickal aspects of the Moon are compassion, fertility, friendships, healing, peace, psychic awareness, purification, and sleep.

The Moon rules Monday, which is an ancient symbol of mystery and peace. Monday is a special day for mothers as the cycle of the moon has long been associated with the female menstrual cycle. Individuals wishing to conceive a baby would be wise to try on a Monday as the magick of motherhood is strong and pregnancy is in the air.

Gender: Feminine

Color: White

Planet: Moon

Element: Water

Energies: Astrology, Children, Dreams/Astral Travel, Emotions, Imagination, Initiation, Magick, New-Age Pursuits, Psychology, Reincarnation, Religion, Short Trips, Spirituality

Tuesday

This is the period of Mars. This day can only always embody the pure strength of the God of War. Spells that are cast on this day are that of energy, force, war and protection.

Gender: Masculine

Color: Red

Planet: Mars

Element: Fire

Energies: Aggression, Business, Beginnings, Combat, Confrontation, Courage, Passion, Partnerships, Sex

Wednesday

Wednesday is controlled by Mercury and devoted to the Teutonic God Odin also known as Woden.

Gender: Masculine

Color: Purple

Planet: Mercury

Element: Air

Energies: Astrology, Communication, Computers, Correspondence, Editing, Healing, Hiring, Legal Appointments, Messages, Music, Signing Contracts, Students, Writing

Thursday

Thursday is the period of Jupiter, the greatest of the planets and suggested to be the most influential. Associated in Norse tradition of Thor, as in Thor's day, spell casters would be prudent to utilize this time for pursuing abundance, prosperity and success spells. Thursday is likewise and some will even affirm that Thor and Jupiter are actually the same embodiment.

Try a short invocation to Jupiter before beginning any ritual on Thursday as a gesture of respect.

Gender: Masculine

Color: Green

Planet: Jupiter

Element: Earth

Energies: Business, Charity, College, Expansion, Gambling, Growth, Law, Luck, Material Wealth, Publishing, Researching, Self-Improvement

Friday

Friday gets its name from the Norse goddess Frigga, the Goddess of Love and Transformation. She rules the divine attitudes of individuals as they manifest on the physical. Because of this, Friday is frequently considered of as unpredictable. Friday has generally been linked to relaxation as it is at the end of the week, but the positive feeling that happens with Friday also has a lot to do with the fact that it is controlled by the planet Venus who is the Goddess of Love. Static relationships and conflicts may be worked out on Fridays with the assist of a spell to Venus and perhaps a small intimate sacrifice. Be careful what you long for on Friday, Venus' eyes could be smiling.

Gender: Feminine

Color: Blue

Planet: Venus

Element: Water

Energies: Affection, Artists, Beauty, Courtship, Friendships, Gardening, Marriage, Music, Partners, Poetry, Relationships, Romantic Love, Shopping, Social Activity

Saturday

Not to anyone's surprise, Saturn rules Saturday. The judgment and the almost crafty nature of Saturn is more obvious on Saturday, which is why it is the perfect day for breaking those pesky habits.

Excellent for banishing spells and clearing old energies. If you have someone that just will not let go of a relationship that you thought was long since dead, give a restriction spell a go next Saturday. Binding spells are also effective on this day. In addition, Saturday is good for concentrating and increasing patience, which is something many witches do not have, myself included.

Gender: Feminine

Color: Black

Planet: Saturn

Element: Fire, Earth

Energies: Binding, Debts, Financing, Hard Work, Housing, Justice, Karma, Limits, Manifestation, Obstacles, Plumbing, Protection, Transformation

10

MAGICKAL COLORS

Red: Energy, Excitement, Power, Passion, Protection, Overcomes Fear, Strength

Blue: Harmony, Loyalty, Astral Travel, Tranquility, Psychic Ability, Integrity, Truth, Meditation, Kindness, Knowledge, Reduces Excess Energy, Relieves Anxiety and Stress, Helps Insomnia

Purple: Blue And Red Energy, Competition, Achieve Work Success, Wealth, Dignity, Control, Respect, Honor, Obedience, Overcome Odds, Command, Court Cases, Awareness, Victory, Blocks Negativity

Pink: Spiritual Love, Romance, Success, Attraction, Compassion, Understanding, Gentleness, Friendship, Forgiveness Self-Love, Self-Respect Heals Broken Hearts, Overcomes Conflict

Orange: Can be substituted for Gold. Success, Emotional Clarity, Control, Happiness, Pleasure, Attracts Luck and Money, Enthusiasm Energy, Hopefulness, Confidence

Yellow: Attraction, Success, Drawing, Communicating, Studying, Memory, Clear Thinking, Decision Making, Confidence

Gold: The Sun. Success, Wealth, Wishes, Happiness

Green: Fertility, Better Business, Creative Ideas, Money, Employment, Rewards, Good Luck, Earth, Plants, Growing

White: All-Purpose Spiritual Awareness and Power. Purity, Truth, Spiritual Devotion, Cooperation, Assistance

Black: Freedom from Evil, Transformation

Silver: Gray Often Used For Silver. Quick Money, Gambling, Moon Magick

Gray: Neutralizes Stress, Negativity, Decreases the Impact of Mistakes, Cleanse Unwanted Energies, Break A Spell of Bad Luck, and Exorcisms

Brown: Consistency, Fertility, Thrift, Work, Awareness, Control, Fruitful, Success in Business, Grounding, Long-Term Achievements, Growth, Determination, Planting

11

HERBS OF THE ZODIAC

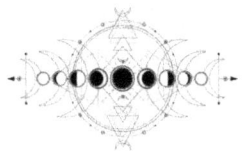

The Zodiac Sign Capricorn falls between the dates of December 22nd to January 19th. This zodiac's herb includes Caraway, Chamomile, Comfrey, Jasmine Marjoram, Rosemary Slippery Elm, Tarragon, and Thyme.

The Zodiac Sign Aquarius falls between the dates of January 20st to February 18th. This zodiac's herb includes Comfrey, Fennel, Frankincense, Myrrh, Peppermint Rosemary, Sandalwood Valerian, and Violet.

The Zodiac Sign Pisces falls between the dates of February 19th to March 20th. This zodiac's herb includes Basil, Borage, Hyacinth, Irish Moss, Lemon Balm, Lovage, Sage, and Willow.

The Zodiac Sign Aries falls between the dates of March 21st to April 19th. This zodiac's herb includes Angelical Root, Basil Chervil, Garlic, Geranium, Hemp, Marjoram, Mustard Seed and Wormwood.

The Zodiac Sign Taurus falls between the dates of April 20th to May 20th. This zodiac's herb includes Catnip Cedar, Colts

Foot, Dandelion, Marsh Mallow Mint Patchouli, Sage, Thyme and Violet.

The Zodiac Sign Gemini falls between the dates of May 21st to June 20th. This zodiac's herb includes Anise, Caraway Seed, Dill, Lavender, Mandrake, Marjoram, Mugwort, Parsley, Vervain, and Wormwood.

The Zodiac Sign Cancer falls between the dates of June 21st to July 22nd. This zodiac's herb includes Aloe, Apple, Bay, Catnip, Geranium Lemon Verbena, Marigold Parsley, and Sage.

The Zodiac Sign Leo falls between the dates of July 23rd to August 22nd. This zodiac's herb includes Anise, Bay Leaves, Chamomile Clove Dill, Eyebright, Lemon Balm, Mint, Oak, Sunflower, and Tarragon.

The Zodiac Sign Virgo falls between the dates of August 23rd to September 22nd. This zodiac's herb includes Caraway Cyprus Dill, Fennel Seed, Horehound, Marjoram, Mint, Skullcap and Valerian.

The Zodiac Sign Libra falls between the dates of September 23rd to October 22nd. This zodiac's herb includes Bergamot Catnip Elderberry, Lemon Verbena, Penny Royal, St. John's Wort and Thyme.

The Zodiac Sign Scorpio falls between the dates of October 23rd to November 21st. This zodiac's herb includes Ash, Basil, Catnip, Coriander, Hops, Horehound, Nettle, Sage, and Sarsaparilla.

The Zodiac Sign Sagittarius falls between the dates of November 22nd to December 21st. This zodiac's herb includes Basil Borage, Burdock, Chervil, Red Clover, Saffron Sage, St. John's Wort and Tobacco.

*Note: The dates may vary by a day or two.

CONCLUSION

Wicca is a recognized religion in the United States. Most states afford Wiccans the day off to celebrate or partake in various Wiccan celebrations and holidays. Even the US Military has started recognizing the Wiccan faith and has Wiccan recruits.

Although Wicca seems more feminine, it is open to all genders and seeks a balance between the feminine and masculine. It is not a religion that will march out and try to convert fresh recruits; instead, it is a belief that allows people to join them of their own free will. Wiccans believe it is not up to them to force a person onto the path of the Wiccan faith. If it is meant to be, a person will eventually find their way to the faith when they are ready.

Although the Wiccan faith, as we know, it has only been around since the 1950s, Paganism and witchcraft have been around since Neanderthal times. It is a peaceful religion that respects all other religions, faiths, and above all, the universe.

If you are looking for spiritual insight and feel a pull towards nature, it may just be your soul looking to connect with the

Conclusion

Great Divine.

REFERENCES

Chamberlain, L. (2019). Wicca living. Wicca Living. https://wiccaliving.com/essentials-wicca/

Forms of Wicca and Wiccan traditions. (n.d.). Wicca.Com. https://wicca.com/wicca/wicca-forms.html

Gordon Melton, J. (2018). Wicca | history & beliefs. In Encyclopædia Britannica. https://www.britannica.com/topic/Wicca

Importance of Nature in Wicca and in Life. (n.d.). Wicca Movement. https://wiccamovement.com/pages/importance-of-nature-in-wicca-and-life-in-general

K, K. (2018, August 22). What is a pentacle or pentagram? | pentacle meaning & pentagram meaning in Wicca. Woot & Hammy. https://wootandhammy.com/blogs/news/what-is-a-pentacle-or-pentagram-meaning-wicca-five-pointed-upside-down-star-protection-symbol

National Geographic Society. (2012, April 13). Hominin history. National Geographic Society. https://www.nationalgeographic.org/media/hominin-history/

Obringer, L. A. (2004, October 29). How witchcraft works. HowStuffWorks. https://people.howstuffworks.com/witchcraft.htm

Perkins, M. (2019, April 5). What is Animism? Learn Religions. https://www.learnreligions.com/what-is-animism-4588366

Pollux, A. (2019, September 27). Who are the Wiccan Gods? Your easy guide to Wiccan deities. Welcome To Wicca Now. https://wiccanow.com/who-is-a-wiccan-god-your-guide-to-wiccan-deities/

Rose, E. (n.d.). MIM. Messages in the Moonlight. https://www.moonlightmessages.com/home

Sage Wright, M. (2013, December 12). Wiccan views on life after death. Exemplore. https://exemplore.com/wicca-witchcraft/Wiccan-Views-on-Life-After-Death

Wigington, P. (2018, December 23). What is the Wiccan rede? Learn Religions. https://www.learnreligions.com/the-wiccan-rede-2562601

Wigington, P. (2019, June 25). Can men be Wiccan too? Of course, they can! Learn Religions. https://www.learnreligions.com/can-men-be-pagan-or-wiccan-2561834

Wigington, P. (2020, January 12). Wicca, witchcraft, or Paganism - what's the difference? Learn Religions. https://www.learnreligions.com/wicca-witchcraft-or-paganism-2562823

Witchcraft, Wicca, and Paganism - what's the difference? (2018, December 13). Blessed Be Magick. https://blessedbemagick.com/blogs/news/witchcraft-wicca-and-paganism-what-s-the-difference

Zilber, A. (2018, November 19). Number of Americans practicing witchcraft estimated to be 1.5 million. Mail Online.

https://www.dailymail.co.uk/news/article-6404733/Number-Americans-practice-witchcraft-estimated-high-1-5-MILLION.html

ABOUT THE AUTHOR

Monique Joiner Siedlak: Author, Witch, Warrior.

With storytelling infused with mysticism, modern paganism, and new age spirituality, Monique awakens your potential. Initiated into the craft at 20, her 80+ books explore the magick and mysteries of life.

A Long Island native, she now calls Southeast Poland home but remains a citizen of Mother Earth.

Beyond her pen, Monique craves new experiences and cherishes nature, advocating for animal welfare.

Join her captivating journey as she transports you to enchanting realms and empowers your own transformative path. Unleash the dormant magic within and embrace the extraordinary with Monique Joiner Siedlak's evocative words.

To find out more about Monique artistically, spiritually, and personally, feel free to visit her **official website.**

www.mojosiedlak.com

facebook.com/mojosiedlak
x.com/mojosiedlak
instagram.com/mojosiedlak
youtube.com/@MoniqueJoinerSiedlak_Author
tiktok.com/@mojosiedlak
bookbub.com/authors/monique-joiner-siedlak
pinterest.com/mojosiedlak

MORE BOOKS BY MONIQUE

African Spirituality Beliefs and Practices

Hoodoo

Seven African Powers: The Orishas

Cooking for the Orishas

Lucumi: The Ways of Santeria

Voodoo of Louisiana

Haitian Vodou

Orishas of Trinidad

Connecting with your Ancestors

Blood Magick

The Orishas

Vodun: West Africa's Spiritual Life

Marie Laveau: Life of a Voodoo Queen

Candomblé: Dancing for the God

Umbanda

Exploring the Rich and Diverse World

Divination Magic for Beginners

Divination with Runes

Divination with Diloggún

Divination with Osteomancy

Divination with the Tarot

Divination with Stones

The Beginner's Guide to Inner Growth

Astral Projection for Beginners

Meditation for Beginners

Reiki for Beginners

Mastering Your Inner Potential

Creative Visualization

Manifesting With the Law of Attraction

Holistic Healing and Energy

Healing Animals with Reiki

Crystal Healing

Communicating with Your Spirit Guides

Empathic Understanding and Enlightenment

Being an Empath Today

Life on Fire

Healing Your Inner Child

Change Your Life

Raising Your Vibe

The Indie Author's Guides

The Indie Author's Guide to Fast Drafting Your Novel

Get a Handle on Life

Get a Handle on Stress

Time Bound

Get a Handle on Anxiety

Get a Handle on Depression

Get a Handle on Procrastination

The Holistic Yoga and Wellness Series

Yoga for Beginners

Yoga for Stress

Yoga for Back Pain

Yoga for Weight Loss

Yoga for Flexibility

Yoga for Advanced Beginners

Yoga for Fitness

Yoga for Runners

Yoga for Energy

Yoga for Your Sex Life

Yoga to Beat Depression and Anxiety

Yoga for Menstruation

Yoga to Detox Your Body

Yoga to Tone Your Body

The DIY Body Care Series

Creating Your Own Body Butter

Creating Your Own Body Scrub

Creating Your Own Body Spray

SUPPORT ME BY LEAVING A REVIEW!

★★★★★

goodreads

www.ingramcontent.com/pod-product-compliance
Lightning Source LLC
Chambersburg PA
CBHW071330040426
42444CB00009B/2120